Classic Cock
and Retro Bart

Cocktails: How

An 1898 Bartender's Guide

Livermore & Knight

Historic Cookbooks of the World
Kalevala Books, Chicago

"Drink because you are happy, but never because you are miserable."
— G.K. Chesterton, 1874–1936

Cocktails: How to Make Them
An 1898 Bartender's Guide

Joanne Asala, Series Editor

Classic Cocktail Guides and Retro Bartender Books and *Historic Cookbooks of the World* are published by Kalevala Books, an imprint of Compass Rose Technologies, Inc. Titles published by Kalevala Books are available at special quantity discounts to use as premiums and sales promotions or for academic use. For more information, please e-mail us at editor@compassrose.com or write to:

Compass Rose Technologies, Inc.
PO Box 409095
Chicago, IL 60640

Editors' Note

Some ingredients found in vintage cocktail guides are unavailable or hard to come by today. Check out our resource guide at the back for vendors who specialize in hard-to-find ingredients and websites with information on how to recreate classic cocktails and cocktail ingredients.

ISBN: 978-1-880954-35-5

Cocktails

COCKTAILS

.. HOW TO MAKE THEM ..

. . . . .

"Inasmuch as you will do this thing, it is best that
you do it intelligently."

. . . . .

PROVIDENCE :
LIVERMORE & KNIGHT CO.
1898

Classic Cocktail Guides and Retro Bartender Books

.. Index ..

A COCKTAIL is an appetizer or stomach stimulant and differs from other drinks in that it is supposed to contain Bitters.

It is the purpose of this book to give the rules for the mixing of simple and well-known cocktails. As to rules for fancy cocktails there is no end, and the addition of the various ingredients for sweetening and blending of fancy cocktails has been left to the taste of the mixer.

A dry cocktail is one in which very little, if any, sweetening is used, and is best for people who are constrained as to the use of sweets.

Cocktails should always be made in a glass with cracked ice, stirred with a spoon, and sufficient ice should be used so that when the drink is served the melting of the ice will cause the drink to be at least one-third water. The finer the ice the quicker it dissolves in the liquor, and hence the colder the drink.

A cocktail should never be bottled and should always be made at the time of drinking. A bottled cocktail might be likened

8

unto a depot sandwich—neither are fit for use except in case of necessity.

The original cocktails were all made from Gin, Whiskey or Brandy, and these are the spirits used in almost every well-known cocktail made to-day. The addition of Vermouth was the first move toward the blending of cocktails and was the initial feature that led to their popularity.

The measures referred to, namely, a mixing-glass, a jigger, and a pony, hold the following quantities :

A mixing glass holds 12 ounces, 6 jiggers, or 24 medium size tablespoonfuls.

A jigger referred to in these rules holds 2 ounces, or 4 medium size tablespoonfuls.

A pony holds 1 ounce, or half a jigger, or 2 tablespoonfuls.

The formulas are simple, practical, easy to follow, and the ingredients are embraced within the contents of the sideboard of the average well-regulated household.

The cherry preserved in Maraschino and the small green olive are often dropped in the bottom of the cocktail glass. As to whether the cherry or olive be used, it is a matter of taste, but on general principles the cherry should go with the sweet drink and the olive with the dry. Neither the cherry nor the olive should ever be served with the drink without first learning whether it is desired or not.

An old-fashioned yet attractive way of serving a cocktail to ladies is the wiping of the rim of the cocktail glass with lemon peel and then dipping the rim in powdered sugar, which leaves a frosty decoration on the rim of the glass.

11

Angostura Bitters may be used in place of Boker's where mentioned in these rules, if preferred, but never more than one-half the quantity.

Orange Bitters may be used in conjunction with the other bitters mentioned, or alone, and the addition of a dash or two, more or less, of these bitters is far from being objectionable, as in the case of the more pungent bitters.

The writer has no caution to give as to any extras that may be added; the only special suggestion he has to offer being—always make cocktails mild and avoid too many bitters.

The tinkle of the ice—the delightful odor of the lemon peel—the fragrance and flavor of this ice-cold appetizer, what an apology it has been for cold soup and over-done entree !

Apple Brandy Cocktail.

A MIXING-GLASS half-full fine ice, two dashes Peyschaud or Boker's bitters, one jigger apple brandy. Mix and strain into a cocktail-glass. Add a piece of twisted lemon peel.

Bitters
Apple Brandy
Lemon peel

Armour Cocktail.

FINE ice in mixing-glass, three dashes orange bitters, half a jigger sherry, half a jigger Italian vermouth. Mix, strain into cocktail-glass. Add a piece of orange peel.

Bitters
Sherry
Italian Vermouth
Orange peel

15

Brandy Cocktail.

Syrup
Bitters
Brandy
Lemon peel

A MIXING-GLASS half-full fine ice, two dashes gum-syrup, two dashes Peyschaud or Boker's bitters, one jigger brandy. Mix and strain into cocktail-glass. Add a piece twisted lemon peel.

Brandy Cocktail—Old-Fashioned.

Sugar
Bitters
Lemon peel
Brandy

C RUSH lump of sugar in a whiskey-glass with sufficient hot water to cover the sugar, add one lump ice, two dashes bitters, a small piece lemon peel, one jigger brandy. Stir with small bar-spoon. Serve leaving spoon in the glass.

16

Brandy Cocktail—Fancy.

FILL a mixing-glass half-full fine ice, add three dashes Maraschino, two dashes Peyschaud or Boker's bitters, one jigger brandy, one dash orange bitters. Mix. Strain into cocktail-glass, the rim of which has been moistened with a piece of lemon and dipped in powdered sugar.

Maraschino
Bitters
Brandy
Lemon
Sugar

Brant Cocktail.

MIXING-GLASS half-full fine ice, two dashes Angostura bitters, one-third of a jigger White Crème de menthe, two-thirds of a jigger brandy. Mix well. Strain into cocktail-glass; twist a piece of lemon peel over the top.

Bitters
Crème de menthe
Brandy
Lemon peel

17

Brown Cocktail.

Bitters
Holland Gin
French Vermouth
Lemon peel

FILL mixing-glass half-full fine ice, add three dashes Boker's bitters, one-half jigger Holland gin, one-half jigger French vermouth; shake until cold. Strain into cocktail-glass; twist a small piece lemon peel on top.

Calasaya Cocktail.

Calasaya
Whiskey
Lemon peel

HALF a jigger Calasaya, half a jigger whiskey, one small piece lemon peel, half a mixing-glass full fine ice. Mix well and strain into a cocktail-glass.

Classic Cocktail Guides and Retro Bartender Books

Country Cocktail.

A MIXING-GLASS half-full fine ice, two dashes of orange bitters, two dashes Boker's bitters, one piece lemon peel, one jigger rye whiskey—no sweetening. Mix and strain into a cocktail-glass.

Bitters
Lemon peel
Whiskey

Champagne Cocktail.

P UT into a long thin glass one lump cut-loaf sugar saturated with Boker's bitters, add one lump of ice, a fair sized piece of lemon peel; fill the glass three-fourths full cold champagne. Stir with spoon and serve.

Sugar
Bitters
Lemon peel
Champagne

19

Champagne Cocktail—Fancy.

Sugar
Bitters
Lemon
Champagne

INTO a long thin glass, put two lumps of sugar; wet one of the lumps with Peyschaud bitters. Add three lumps of ice and the rind of a lemon. Catch one end of the lemon rind on the edge of the glass. Fill the glass nearly full with cold champagne. Stir with a bar-spoon and serve.

Chocolate Cocktail.

Egg
Bitters
Port wine
Sugar

BREAK a fresh egg into a mixing-glass, half full fine ice, add one dash bitters, one jigger port wine, one teaspoonful fine sugar. Shake well and strain into a cocktail-glass.

20

Classic Cocktail Guides and Retro Bartender Books

Cider Cocktail.

SATURATE a lump of cut-loaf sugar with Boker's bitters. Place it, with one lump of ice and a small piece of lemon peel, in a thin cider-glass, then fill up with cold cider. Stir with spoon and serve.

Sugar
Bitters
Lemon peel
Cider

Clam Cocktail.

PUT into a large cocktail-glass a half-dozen little-neck clams with all their liquor, season with pepper and salt to taste; add two dashes lemon-juice, one dash Tobasco sauce, and a very little cayenne pepper. Serve with small fork or spoon in glass.

Clams
Lemon juice
Tobasco sauce

21

Coffee Cocktail.

Sugar
Egg
Port wine
Brandy

FILL a mixing-glass half-full of fine ice; add one teaspoonful of powdered white sugar, one fresh egg, one pony port wine, one pony of brandy. Shake thoroughly and strain into a large cocktail-glass. Grate a little nutmeg on top before serving.

Gin Cocktail—Holland.

Bitters
Syrup
Holland Gin
Lemon peel

MIXING-GLASS half-full fine ice, two dashes Boker's or Peyschaud bitters, two dashes gum-syrup, one jigger Holland gin. Mix; strain into a cocktail-glass. Add a piece of twisted lemon peel.

22

Gin Cocktail—Old-Fashioned Holland.

PUT a lump of sugar in a whiskey glass; add enough hot water to cover the sugar. Crush the sugar; add a lump of ice, two dashes Boker's bitters, small piece of lemon peel, one jigger of Holland gin. Mix with small bar-spoon and serve with spoon in glass.

Sugar
Bitters
Lemon peel
Holland Gin

Gin Cocktail—Plymouth.

MIXING-GLASS half-full fine ice, three dashes orange or Peyschaud bitters, one jigger Plymouth gin. Mix well, strain into cocktail-glass. Add a small piece lemon peel.

Bitters
Plymouth Gin
Lemon peel

23

Gin Cocktail—Tom.

Bitters
Tom Gin
Lemon peel

HAVE mixing-glass half-full fine ice; add two dashes Peyschaud or Boker's bitters, one jigger Tom gin. Mix well, strain into cocktail-glass and add a small piece of lemon peel.

Gin Cocktail—Old-Fashioned Tom.

Sugar
Bitters
Lemon peel
Tom Gin

MIX same as Old Fashioned Holland Gin Cocktail, using Old Tom gin in place of Holland.

24

Harvard Cocktail.

MIXING-GLASS half-full of fine ice; one dash gum-syrup, three dashes Boker's bitters, half a jigger Italian vermouth, half a jigger of brandy. Mix and strain into a cocktail-glass, then fill up with seltzer and serve quickly.

Syrup
Bitters
Italian Vermouth
Brandy
Seltzer

Irish Cocktail.

MIXING-GLASS half-full fine ice, three dashes orange bitters, two dashes Horsford's acid phosphate, one-half jigger whiskey, one-half jigger Italian vermouth. Mix well, strain into cocktail-glass.

Bitters
Acid phosphate
Whiskey
Italian Vermouth

25

Jamaica Rum Cocktail.

Syrup
Bitters
Jamaica Rum
Lemon peel

MIXING-GLASS half-full fine ice, two dashes gum-syrup, two dashes orange bitters, two dashes Boker's bitters, one jigger Jamaica rum. Mix and strain into cocktail-glass. Add a small piece twisted lemon peel.

Jersey Cocktail.

Sugar
Bitters
Lemon peel
Cider

PUT one lump of ice in thin cider-glass. Add one-half tablespoonful fine sugar, two dashes Boker's bitters, one piece lemon peel. Fill up with cold cider. Stir well, and drink while effervescent.

26

Liberal Cocktail.

FILL a mixing-glass half-full fine ice, add one dash syrup, half a jigger Picon bitters, half a jigger whiskey. Mix, strain into cocktail-glass. A small piece of lemon peel on top.

Syrup
Bitters
Whiskey
Lemon peel

Manhattan Cocktail.

FILL mixing-glass half-full fine ice, add two dashes gum-syrup, two dashes Boker's bitters, one-half jigger Italian vermouth, one-half jigger whiskey. Mix, strain into cocktail-glass. Add a piece of lemon peel.

Syrup
Bitters
Italian Vermouth
Whiskey
Lemon peel

27

Manhattan Cocktail----Dry.

Bitters
Italian Vermouth
Whiskey
Lemon peel

PREPARE same as Manhattan Cocktail, leaving out syrup.

Manhattan Cocktail—Extra Dry.

Bitters
French Vermouth
Whiskey
Lemon peel

MIX same as Manhattan Cocktail. Leave out syrup, and use French vermouth in place of Italian.

28

Marguerite Cocktail.

HALF a mixing-glass full of fine ice, three dashes of orange bitters, one-half jigger of Plymouth gin, one-half jigger of French vermouth. Mix, strain into cocktail-glass. Place an olive in the bottom of glass and serve.

Bitters
Plymouth Gin
French Vermouth

Martini Cocktail—No. 1.

HALF a mixing-glass full fine ice, three dashes orange bitters, one-half jigger Tom gin, one-half jigger Italian vermouth, a piece lemon peel. Mix, strain into cocktail-glass.

Bitters
Gin
Italian Vermouth
Lemon peel

29

Martini Cocktail—No. 2.

Bitters
Tom Gin
Italian Vermouth
Sherry
Lemon peel

FILL mixing-glass half-full fine ice. Add two dashes Boker's bitters, one-half jigger Tom gin, one-half jigger Italian vermouth, half a teaspoonful sherry, piece of lemon peel. Mix, and strain into cocktail-glass.

Medford Rum Cocktail.

Syrup
Bitters
Medford Rum
Lemon peel

HAVE mixing-glass half-full fine ice. Add dash gum-syrup, two dashes Boker's bitters, one jigger Medford rum. Mix and strain into cocktail-glass. Add a piece of twisted lemon peel.

30

Metropole Cocktail.

HAVE a mixing-glass half-full fine ice, add two dashes gum-syrup, two dashes Peyschaud bitters, one dash orange bitters, half a jigger brandy, half a jigger French vermouth. Mix, strain into cocktail-glass, add small piece twisted lemon peel.

Syrup
Bitters
Brandy
French Vermouth
Lemon peel

Metropolitan Cocktail.

TWO lumps of ice in a small wine-glass, add three dashes gum-syrup, two dashes Boker's bitters, one pony brandy, one pony French vermouth. Mix, take out the ice, add a small piece twisted lemon peel.

Syrup
Bitters
Brandy
French Vermouth
Lemon peel

31

Oyster Cocktail.

Lemon juice
Tobasco Sauce
Tomato Catsup
Oysters

A FEW dashes lemon juice in a tumbler, add a dash of Tobasco sauce, a teaspoonful of vinegar, a few dashes tomato catsup, six Blue Point oysters, with all their liquor; season to taste with pepper and salt. Mix and serve with small fork or spoon in the glass.

Princeton Cocktail.

Bitters
Tom Gin
Port wine

A MIXING-GLASS half-full fine ice, three dashes orange bitters, one and a half pony Tom gin. Mix, strain into cocktail-glass; add half a pony port wine carefully and let it settle in bottom of cocktail before serving.

Classic Cocktail Guides and Retro Bartender Books

Riding Club Cocktail.

MIXING-GLASS half-full fine ice, one dash Angostura bitters, a small bar-spoonful Horsford's Acid Phosphate, one jigger Calasaya. Mix and strain into cocktail-glass.

Bitters
Acid phosphate
Calasaya

Rob Roy Cocktail.

FILL a mixing-glass half-full fine ice. Add two dashes Boker's bitters, one-half jigger Scotch whiskey, one-half jigger Italian vermouth. Mix and strain into cocktail-glass. Place a small piece lemon peel on top.

Bitters
Scotch Whiskey
Italian Vermouth
Lemon peel

33

Soda Cocktail.

Sugar
Bitters
Lemon peel
Soda

ONE teaspoonful fine sugar in a large bar-glass, one lump of ice, three dashes Peyschaud bitters, one piece lemon peel; add one bottle of plain or lemon soda. Mix and drink during effervescence.

Star Cocktail.

Syrup
Bitters
Brandy
Italian Vermouth
Lemon peel

FILL a mixing-glass half-full fine ice, add two dashes gum-syrup, three dashes Peyschaud or Boker's bitters, one-half jigger apple brandy, one-half jigger Italian vermouth. Mix, strain into cocktail-glass, twist small piece lemon peel on top.

34

Turf Cocktail.

ONE dash Angostura bitters, three dashes orange bitters, one jigger Tom gin in a mixing-glass half-full fine ice. Mix, strain into cocktail-glass; add a piece twisted lemon peel.

Bitters
Tom Gin
Lemon peel

Vermouth Cocktail.

MIXING-GLASS half-full fine ice, two dashes Boker's or Peyschaud bitters, one jigger Italian vermouth. Mix well, strain into cocktail-glass; add a piece lemon peel.

Bitters
Italian Vermouth
Lemon peel

35

Vermouth Cocktail—Dry.

Bitters
French Vermouth
Lemon peel

PREPARE same as Vermouth Cocktail, using French vermouth in place of Italian; twist a piece lemon peel over top.

Vermouth Cocktail—Fancy.

Maraschino
Bitters
Italian Vermouth
Lemon peel

HAVE mixing-glass half-full fine ice. Add three dashes Maraschino, two dashes Boker's bitters, one jigger Italian vermouth and one dash orange bitters. Mix and strain into cocktail-glass, the rim of which has been moistened with a piece of lemon peel and dipped in powdered sugar.

36

Vermouth Cocktail—French.

THREE dashes orange bitters in mixing-glass half-full fine ice; add one jigger French vermouth. Mix well, strain into cocktail-glass; add a piece twisted lemon peel on top.

Bitters
French Vermouth
Lemon peel

Whiskey Cocktail.

MIXING-GLASS half-full fine ice, two dashes gum-syrup, two dashes Peyschaud bitters, one jigger whiskey. Mix, strain into cocktail-glass; add a small piece of twisted lemon peel.

Syrup
Bitters
Whiskey
Lemon peel

37

Whiskey Cocktail—Fancy.

Maraschino
Bitters
Whiskey
Lemon peel

HAVE mixing-glass half-full fine ice. Add two dashes Maraschino, two dashes Boker's bitters, one jigger whiskey, one dash orange bitters. Mix until very cold. Strain into cocktail-glass, the rim of which has been moistened with a piece of lemon peel and dipped in powdered sugar.

Whiskey Cocktail—Old-Fashioned.

Sugar
Bitters
Lemon peel
Whiskey

PUT a lump of sugar in a whiskey glass; add enough hot water to cover the sugar. Crush the sugar; add a lump of ice, two dashes Boker's bitters, small piece of lemon peel, one jigger whiskey. Mix with small bar-spoon and serve with spoon in glass.

38

Whiskey Cocktail—New York.

ILL mixing-glass half-full fine ice. Add two dashes Boker's bitters, one-half jigger whiskey, one-half jigger Italian vermouth, half a teaspoonful sherry, piece of lemon peel. Mix, and strain into cocktail-glass.

Bitters
Whiskey
Italian Vermouth
Sherry
Lemon peel

Yale Cocktail.

ILL a mixing-glass half-full fine ice, three dashes orange bitters, one dash Peyschaud bitters, a piece lemon peel, one jigger Tom gin. Mix, strain into cocktail-glass; add a squirt of siphon seltzer.

Bitters
Lemon peel
Tom Gin
Seltzer

39

Classic Cocktail Resource Guide

Some ingredients found in vintage cocktail guides are unavailable or hard to come by today. However, the creation of historically accurate cocktails is a growing hobby and with a bit of Internet research, you will find recipes for bitters and syrups online, as well as manufacturers that are developing new product lines for the classic cocktail enthusiast.

Vendors

A short selection of online vendors selling bitters, mixers, syrups, wine, liqueurs, and spirits. This list is by no means complete but is a good place to start your search.

BevMo!
www.bevmo.com

Binny's Beverage Depot
www.binnys.com

The Bitter Truth
www.the-bitter-truth.com

Cocktail Kingdom
www.cocktailkingdom.com

Fee Brothers
www.feebrothers.com

Hi-Time Wine Cellars
www.hitimewine.net

Internet Wines and Spirits
www.internetwines.com

The Jug Shop
www.thejugshop.com

Monin Gourmet Flavorings
www.moninstore.com

The Whiskey Exchange
www.thewhiskyexchange.com

General Interest

These sites provide background information on individual ingredients, suggestions for substitutes, current commercial availability, and recipes.

The Chanticleer Society
A Worldwide Organization of Cocktail Enthusiasts
www.chanticleersociety.org

Drink Boy
Adventures in Cocktails
www.drinkboy.com

The Internet Cocktail Database Ingredients Search
www.cocktaildb.com/ingr_search

Museum of the American Cocktail
www.museumoftheamericancocktail.org

WebTender Wiki
www.wiki.webtender.com

Coming Soon from
Classic Cocktail Guides
and Retro Bartender Books

Home Made
Beverages

The Manufacture of Non-Alcoholic and
Alcoholic Drinks in the Household, Including
Recipes for Essences, Extracts, and Syrups

A Pre-Prohibition Cocktail Book

Albert Hopkins

Classic Cocktail Guides
and Retro Bartender Books

Nineteenth-Century Cocktail Creations

How to Mix Drinks: A Bar Keeper's Handbook

George Winter

ISBN: 978-1-880954-30-0

Jack's Manual of Recipes for Fancy Mixed Drinks and How to Serve Them

A Pre-Prohibition Cocktail Book

J. A. Grohusko

ISBN: 978-1-880954-28-7

Stuart's Fancy Drinks and How to Mix Them

Containing Clear and Practical Directions for
Mixing All Kinds of Cocktails, Sours, Egg Nog,
Sherry Cobblers, Coolers, Absinthe, Crustas,
Fizzes, Flips, Juleps, Fixes, Punches, Lemonades,
Pousse Cafes, Invalids' Drinks, Etc. Etc.

Thomas Stuart

ISBN: 978-1-880954-34-8

Classic Cocktail Guides
and Retro Bartender Books

What to Drink

Non-Alcoholic Drinks and Cocktails
Served During Prohibition

Bertha E. L. Stockbridge

ISBN: 978-1-880954-36-2

Printed in Great Britain
by Amazon